RECKLESS LOVELY

MARTHA SILANO

saturnalia books

Distributed by University Press of New England
Hanover and London

Saturnalia Books
105 Woodside Rd.
Ardmore, PA 19003
info@saturnaliabooks.com

ISBN: 978-0-9899797-1-9
Library of Congress Control Number: 2013951638

Book Design by Saturnalia Books
Printing by Westcan Printing Group, Canada

Author Photo: Langdon Cook

Distributed by:
University Press of New England
1 Court Street
Lebanon, NH 03766
800-421-1561

Sincere thanks the editors of the following publications for selecting the following poems for publication, a few in slightly different versions:

The Cincinnati Review: "Ode to Mystery"; *Crab Creek Review*: "Ode to Artichokes"; *Drunken Boat*: "Summons and Petition for a Name Change"; *Ecotone*: "Flower Girl"; *Filter*: "Right about now"; *The Journal*: "House of Mystery," "Constellation"; *The Kenyon Review Online*: "Hope is the Thing With"; "The Poet is the Priest of the Invisible"; *The Laurel Review*: "Black Holes"; *Mobile City*: "Pry Bar Constellation"; *North American Review*: "Pale Blue Dot"; *Poetry Northwest*: "The Untied States of America"; *The Poet's Market 2014*: "Recipe"; *Ploughshares*: "Wolves Keep in Touch by Howling"; *Prairie Schooner*: "How to Read Italian Renaissance Painting," "Easter Drama"; *Rattle*: "La Gioconda"; *Redactions*: "Size"; *Southern Humanities Review*: "Saint Catherine of Siena," "Appropriate Incongruities"; *Sou'wester*: "Damage Status"; *Terrain.org*: "God in Utah," "If You Could Be Anybody, Who Would You Be?"; *Voices in Italian Americana*: "Leonardo DaVinci's Gran Cavallo," "We Found Martha Silano!"

"Size" is reprinted in the *Here, There, and Everywhere: Redmond Association of Spokenword Anthology*.

I am grateful to the following organizations for providing me much needed time in quiet, peaceful, exceedingly productive settings:

The Helene Rubioff Whiteley Center
Kangaroo B&B / Artsmith
Seattle 4Culture
Camac Centre D'Art

Sincere gratitude to the following for their unflagging support and editorial prowess: Susan Blackwell Ramsey, Erin Malone, Stacey Luftig, Kelli Russell Agodon, Molly Tenenbaum, Moira Linehan, and Tina Kelley.

Sincere gratitude for the guidance, patience, and beautiful work of Henry Israeli and Sarah Blake, editor and assistant editor at Saturnalia Books.

For his genius and geniality, I remain incomparably indebted to Rex Gentry, MD.

This book is for Langdon – Body my house / my horse my hound . . .

TABLE OF CONTENTS

I.

THE BIG BANG

begins with a dash of giant impact, a sprinkling
of moonlets, pinch of heavy bombardment.

Sift in crusty iron sulfide, fricasseed stromatolites,
one level teaspoon cyanobacteria. Slowly dribble

ammonia, methane, hydrogen; drop a dollop
of ocean. Chill this velvety soup, cream

congealing in a Protozoic freezer.
Mix well your deep hypothermal marine.

Let go your nucleus, embrace your blue-green,
equal parts cointreau/cran-raz (let's call it

sunset). After the foaming, beat in trilobites—
highly spiny, highly spiffy. After the rising,

serve on a plate of sand where a horseshoe crab
exudes 60,000 eggs. With your baster, tickle

its telson, its pedipalps. Brush
with a muddy glaze. Reserve.

Go kolacky, go goo-goo for *Siphusactum*
gregarium goulash, bonkers for sponge.

Do that thing you do with disambiguation,
with cartilage and dip, with molting.

Give it that ol' placoderm shaping
till it's time to roll out the lobe-fins,

to pack this floating island brachiopodishly,
to get this ocean fizz fizzing, this volcano

revolting. Hurry up that Hurry-up Gravy,
festoon Pangea with gingko dainties,

headlong into the dark, dark fast-
fudge Black Gold Betty, which is always

nipping at the heels of the collembola
crepes, the fairy shrimp consommé.

In go the hexapods! (Goodbye, gill branches!)
Fire up that grill; make way for metamorphosis,

for 10,000 blooming delphiniums, for Liopleurodon
and Megatherium—for the nimble Hagerman Horse,

for the leg of lamb in a wire basket, spitting and hissing.

BLACK HOLES

Those pink splotches up there on the planetarium ceiling? What happens when fusion ceases and gravity wins, the lighter stuff spewing in all directions, winding up as craneflies and shrews, the big stuff collapsing, reducing down to a dark pumpernickel loaf the baker neglected to knead. Challah's much less dense—light escapes. Same goes for Wonder Bread. Our sun is smaller, a golden brioche, its hydrogen good for another billion years. If you get too close to a black hole's horizon, your feet become spaghetti, your torso linguini, your head a strand of capellini. As you slip into a cauldron of bubbling blackness, note the slurping. You will disappear and you will not return, especially not through a portal to a fancier table setting, cannoli flown direct from Palermo. All of this has something to do with a capsule, a Cape, with the bending of light, with Einstein. To rid yourself of gravitational pull, blast off at a rate of seven miles per second. If you want a parking space in front of the Air & Space Museum, cram yourself down to the size of a ciliegene. As Mick Jagger says, paint it black, or get thee a shroud to shield thyself from lightlessness. When someone says hello, say: gravity is just the curvature of space and time, say: I'm a burnt Italian pizza. The black hole in Sagittarius doesn't ask how it got to be four million times the size of the sun. Do you often misplace your cell phone, wallet, keys? No need to worry because at the point of singularity the laws of physics vaporize like your Aunt Josephine's eggplant parmigiana. It reminds me of the summer I tried to learn a foreign language, feeling all wow, when really I knew about fifteen words: *Por favore, un mezzo kilo di pane*, and just like that—thwack of a knife, hunk of crusty bread—the same way I'm telling you now there's no escape.

SIZE

What she thought was large—a 64-ounce Big Gulp,
boxcars creaking from one end of town to the other,

Jupiter's red spot, the silvery, sweeping pinwheel galaxy —
are tinier than the tiniest bone in a pygmy shrew.

Big, it turns out, is 300,000 light-years wide,
a dark corona surrounding the Milky Way,

which it wears like the halo of an angel
in mourning, a cloud-like penumbra, a gypsy's

funereal kerchief ten times the size of every visible star,
every trace of dust, gasp of gas, each planetary speck.

Try that on for size. Try on the black *babushka*
beyond which everything else is shroud-less mycoplasma.

This is the size of her thoughts as she walks down row after row
at the Tomb of the Unknowns, lowers her uncloaked head.

PRY BAR CONSTELLATION

At the planetarium the docent aimed her light-up pointer at three stars.
This is the Pry Bar Constellation, she said. This is how the mummies

spoke to Osiris, their gauzy mouths pried open like cans
of black olives. But when I Googled *Egyptian astronomy*

I got nothing—not the Imperishables, stars that do not rise
or set in the land of the Sphinx, not the story about the crown

of Sah, which they rode for seventy days to the Underworld,
sort of like Egyptian Persephones, returning for the flooding

of the Nile. What I'd like to see is a green-backed heron wading
in the Nile. What I'd like to say is that the mummification—

bicarbonate, chloride, sodium, sulfate, honey and wine, oil of borage,
liver and lungs packed in salt, the body covered in natron for forty days,

the brain removed through the nostrils with a single curved hook—
makes me very tired, or maybe it's that hot, dry 100-mile journey

to a hidden cave, slaves dragging those impossibly sturdy tombs,
those libation dishes, spoonbill-adorned hair combs, tusk figurines

and recumbent lions, extravagance beyond measure heading
for the dark. I guess I'm lucky I'm not an Egyptologist, white-toga

and sandal clad, deciphering hieroglyphics, because then I'd be the one
who squealed on those who stumbled on the spoils. I wonder

if she made up the part about the pry bar, but really how much stranger
is it than a sky replete with a crab, a dragon, two bears, a swan?

Than a club-wielding guy in hot pursuit of a hare, a long band of leather keeping his kilt from falling endlessly through the sky?

ODE TO MYSTERY

and to magic, not magicians with their man-
made manipulations of rabbits and scarves,

of three rings joined then freed, of coins
that disappear/reappear, but the something-

out-of-nothing why of atmosphere, of star fruit,
warthog, and rotifer, extracting minerals

from mountains, refining what's dug up
into wire, so we can gab with Aunt Polly

across the Atlantic, turn what we extract
into steel for ships and girders. Consider

the intricacy of the human eye—rods and cones
trapping photons, sclera sheathing the optic nerve,

vitreous chambers and vascularization, ganglion cells
and plexiform layers; the ear and its tunnels, its drums:

airflow above and below a wing that equals lift,
power of a motor measured in horses, precision

of a peregrine knocking pigeons from the sky,
uncanny usefulness of yeast—bread broken

at the hearth, at the hallowed screen. O symmetry
of equations! Equal signs denoting equality!

Mystery of spiraling nautilids, benthic
tubeworms, swinging-both-ways squid.

O humans and their enormous heads barely
eking through the canal, anointing each other

genius when clearly paramecium deserve the laurels.
Mystery of nematodes bravely clinging as they take

their snaky ride not unlike a tunneled, caustic waterslide—
circular, orificial. Who really deserves the shiny trophy:

we, who launch our dinghies into the roaring unknown,
or the barnacles hunkering down for their twice-daily

drought? Language is spiffy, but lo the hocus-pocus
of pheromones, crickets and cockroaches emitting

lickable seductions. That anything lives at all, that fog
rolls in and out, that milk spurts from the teat, that laughter

erupts when the child reads *buc-a-BAC, buc-a-BAC,*
and the boy in the story tucks his chicken into bed.

PALE BLUE DOT

Candice Hansen-Koharcheck, I'm not sure how
to pronounce your name, but you were the first

to spot it, this two-pixel speck otherwise known
as planet Earth. Sitting at your screen, shades drawn,

office dark, you searched the digital photos sent back
by Voyager 1, four billion miles from your desk.

And there it was, not the big blue marble swirling
with clouds and continents, not the one Apollo astronauts

the sheer beauty brought tears—thanking God and America,
declaring no need to fight over borders or oil; this was not

that view; this was how our planet might look to an alien.
And yet how close this photo came to not being taken at all;

scientists arguing aiming the camera back at the sun
might fry the lens, questioning the worth of such a risk;

this shot you say still gives you chills, dear Candice,
our planet bathed in the spacecraft's reflective light.

Pale blue dot lit by a glowing beam: I'm surprised
Christians didn't have a hey day, though viewing

His crowning achievement requires squinting.
When NASA put it on display at the Jet Propulsion Lab,

a blow-up print spanning fourteen feet, visitors touched
the pinprick so often the image needed constant replacing,

perhaps because without the little arrow we wouldn't know
which pinprick was home. And yet its barely-there-ness

doesn't excuse the plastic bags, duct tape, juice packs,
sweat pants that lodge in the stomachs of whales. And yet

its lack of distinction doesn't pardon the brown-pudding goop
on the Gulf of Mexico's floor, a goop in which nothing alive

has been found. To reckon that speck, mourn the loss
of the black torrent toad. To take it in, grasp its full weight,

then turn toward a child's insistent *give me a ride in a rocket ship!
With meteors and turbulence!* Like you, dear Candice, alone

and in the dark while a loved one's asking *Where are you going?
When are you coming back?*

DAMAGE STATUS

after Gwendolyn Brooks

My polonium, your magnetism. My governess, my garret; your Rue Cuvier,
your aromatic woods. Me: the stilled flickering stars; you: feverish heat; us:
opposite of stilted, a French-windowed Fontainebleau, tourmaline and topaz,
main-squeezing quartz, or let's math it: tight quarters equal high-frequency
vibrations. We vowed in lovely blue with bicycles, with heather and gorse,
returned to the lab, to X, and the loves kept coming—the unborn/unknown
balancing the known. My constant current, your unchangeable. My pitchblende,
my nameless, our 1/10-gram proof; your tumults, our intermingled script.
What gleaming! What fission! What detonation (your/my prize). Anemia,
hysteria, sexual decline: the things we Curies would cure! Marriages that strain
breath, burn skin, glow with flowering failure. Chain reaction of aches.

CONSTELLATION

Because I stole the horse's reins,
my gelding elicits a still-tail silence.

Because silence is a constant,
the loon will not call, the lens

bears down on a looted nest.
Soon the net, soon enlisted

to sorrow. Soon a ton of solo,
Leo called into action.

The stolen, the loosened,
I'm nil with them, my muzzle

a lost canoe in Orion (oceans
have nothing on Draco,

on Cassiopeia's listing).
Cetus breaches while a saw-whet

*no no no*s. What's the weight
of Cygnus? How long

'til my castles topple, sing
a crash of high-stakes half-

notes? O hydra, O heron, O howling
hound not howling—the whole dang lot

of tinsel and ills, lilt of every living cell.

II.

UNDER THE SUN

there was nothing at all

        nothing

then wingless

        bristled

springtailed

        lacking eyes

antennae

        pigmentation

procreation

        the stringing of sperm

along spun thread

        resembling a clothesline

shiny whip-tailed gifts

        for the lucky gal

who stumbleth upon them

        who after a series

of waltzes and tangos

        tucks them inside her

lays her thirty eggs

        makes for a suitable crevice

There was nothing

        and then I noted

the zygentoma

        atop a small girl's head

was it covered with scales

        not covered with scales

or maybe covered with scales

        (this question I've kept asking)

Molt mate molt mate molt mate

        Nothing

Wingless

        Winged

dragonflies

                    descending on cycads
on sphenopsids
                    while Diplodocus dined on club moss
Wings
                    and the folding of wings
so boring into garage walls
                    taking up house
in abandoned split-levels
                    showy and vulnerable cloaked
exposed shut tightly away
                    like a folded map
the route to Pico de Neblina
                    like an umbrella
on a sunny day
                    paper fan
on the shortest coldest
                    to hunker to hide
to make like a mud wasp
                    to slink inside
ambush later
                    tunnel in and be safe
to poke into nests
                    exist on a diet of stolen beeswax
no more flopped open
                    dumb-luck dependence
and the next day metamorphic
                    in the pages of *Glamour*
rags-to-riches makeover
                    from shit brown
to jungle red elytra
                    of the giraffe-necked weevil
despite the give-or-take
                    fifteen-million year extinction
when adaptive radiation went kaput
                    when most of all that creep-eth

breath-eth buzz-eth

galump-eth sex-eth spar-eth

went AWOL

paving the avenue of asp

the boulevard of bee

hastening

the fecundity of flies

Wings wings more wings

creatures on high

releasing themselves

into cool summer dusk

flutter and lift of stonefly

caddis hatch of your dreams

gnat swarm the envy

of the priest

the bloodthirsty flea

the popping cork

of bubbly wisteria

of carpel carnival

of a petal-ful parade

of locules gone loco

of epigenous euphoria

corollas wide open

for a bee butt's nudge

 pollen smudge

a mucked-up derriere

accidental do-si-do

and the cross-breeding

square dance began

orgy of hybridization

dis and that

this and dat

a quarter million species

of buzz of tubular bliss

all of it something

something quite new

HOW TO READ ITALIAN RENAISSANCE PAINTING

Pay attention to cryptic grapes, wandering
aimless skulls, a robed apostle's vortex

of red. Pay attention to luminous gloom,
to the attention paid to each fold, each leaf,

each angel's blue-tipped wing, to every look
of beseeching dismay. Notice uneasy clouds

to the right, uncertain urns to the left. Notice
theatrical expressions, God diving in to shatter

the silence in Mary's room. Notice shutters
everywhere. Take these to mean the master

is a master of worry. When they say human figure,
think naked man, sometimes with pubic hair,

sometimes not—flawlessness like Jack Lalanne
with a scruffy beard. When they say reclining nude,

think woman with a body like soft Dresden hills,
like challah. The angels always carry large, spiral

candles—the kind burned at funerals—grasped
with two hands (Christ's body confirms this),

spiraling akin to spiraling bodies. Also, bare feet.
Also, exalted pathos. Also, everyone's either

pointing, shadowed, or ineffably smiling. Did I say
confidence? Did I say harmony? Did I say a quilted

sleeve? When the women aren't reclining,
they're a bonneted sweetness, a golden serene.

Meanwhile, those cryptic cherubs; meanwhile
those enigmatically fleeing cats. Seeking aid

she turns to us, but we are helpless with our
fragile hands, our dark, roaming eyes. And though

the ship is inscrutable, the finger: yes. And
though the tension is palpable—in the embrace

of the two pregnant women, in the flourishes
of peasant grief—the book is on the bookstand,

the *sfumato* is *sfumato*-ing, the lute-r is lute-ing,
the baby doesn't tumble from his mother's arms,

the hourglass balances on the stool, does not crash and break.

LA GIOCONDA

I'm deaf, I'm in mourning; I've just had a 2nd child.
I'm toothless, palsied, pregnant, paralyzed.

Clearly, I'm a reflection of the painter's neuroses;
clearly, I have a toothache. Turn the canvas

sideways, at a 45-degree angle. Scan the dark swirls:
and you'll see them, the buffalo and the lion. Twenty

animals in all, including a snake representing
envy, a leopard because its skin kills the wanting

of what we don't have. I'm the Jolly Lady, wife
of Francesco del Giocondo; I'm Lisa (a real-life person);

I'm idealized, the artist's mother, the Madonna (a mule
nestles between my breasts—have you spotted

the ape?) Superimposed on a Chinese landscape,
I'm the eternal female, queen of sepulchral secrets.

My half-smile is the smile of enlightenment,
and those glowing hands? So Buddha. In 1962,

posing with Jackie and JFK, I was valued at $720 million,
six times the price of a Pollock or de Kooning.

Some have said that in my placid eyes tiny letters
and numbers reveal I'm Gian Giamono Caprotti,

my painter's apprentice, but don't buy it.
Forget the theories relating to my lack

of eyebrows and lashes, lost not from plucking
but the ravages of restoration. Housed at Versailles,

entwined myself in the Sun King's cucumber patch,
silently basked in Le Tuileries while Napoleon, quaffing

his coveted Chambertin, scuffed around in beat-up red slippers.
When WW2 broke out, they wrapped me in waterproof paper,

whisked me to a land of poppies and castles. Behind
two layers of bulletproof glass, I live on at the Louvre,

where each year seven million spend an average
of fifteen seconds discerning my ambiguous mood. I'm

unfinished; I've been stuffed beneath a trench coat, smuggled
back to Florence. Doused with acid, stoned, pummeled

with a teacup. Touched-up, varnished, de-varnished, infested
with insects; fumigated. I'm a miasma of optical illusions;

my paint is cracking. My visage excites the random noise
in your visual system; emotion recognition software reveals

I'm 83% happy, 9% disgusted, 6% fearful, two pinches angry,
one iota neutral. You love me like you love your sphinx,

your flying saucers, your Area 51; I'm your koan,
your inscrutable floozy, your syphilitic conundrum,

your angelic aspara, your enduring durga. You're here
because I render you agog, aha-less, uncomfortably mum.

ODE TO FRIDA KAHLO'S EYEBROWS

Cult of the brow ascending like a condor,
of refusal to bow to the whimsy of busy tweezers.
From follicle to follicle, freedom unfurls.
Brow most buxom. Ferret brow.
Brow channeling Hieronymus Boschian shenanigans.
Brow championing Duchampian high jinx.
Brow side-skirting ye olde pot o wax.
Brow hobnobbing with Salvadori Dali's mustache.
Mink stole brow; brow I-stole-it-from-a-rodent.
Brow suggesting a profuse, gargantuan beard.
Circus-circuit brow.
Brow that never shook hands with laser.
Most inexplicable brow, most unpixelated.
Bad luck black kitten brow on the prowl.
Mercury in retrograde brow.
Brow undaunted by a John Deere tractor.
Brow the embodiment of national glory.
Brow the mystic mestiza, but brow also
weeping with dislodged fetus, with loss and forlornness.
Brow a come-hither furry viper.
Brow the little known Black Shag Slug.
Brow the unretractable bewhiskered tongue.
Brow the fleecy fluke, tufted cobra, downy leech.
Brow the dark secret of the fastidiously plucked,
that perpetual raised-brow surprise.
Brow surprising, but unsurprised.
Brow the prismatic lion in the wardrobe when you were expecting beige scarves.
Brow adding a bristly flourish to bright Tehuana dress.
Sing holy praises to the insistence of the brow.
Sit down and write a letter to the core beliefs of the brow.
Knit a sweater to the milagro-like votivity of the brow.

Conjure new words to praise the liftingness of brow.
Flamenco to the mural-worthiness of the brow.
Praise god for the untamability of the brow.
Brow most steadfast. Brow on endless loop,
brow most perennial, most acanthus.
Brow aching yet soaring like an unruffled raven.
Unamputated brow.
Brow never renouncing its femininity.
Feminine brow donning its midnight suit.
Brow the corpse that proves the path to the next.
Brow never resting in peace.
Long live the flourish of the stalwart, seaward sooty gull in every self-portrait.
Long live the childlike exuberance of the feisty, the feral. Long live the monkeys
and parrots, perched beside the unwieldy, the emblematic.
Long live those wooly-bear wonders worthy of worship, like two black wings—
signature smudges left by the pig twirling on a spit
todas las dias, todas las noches.

MYSTERY OF THE BRA

I nearly tripped over as I jogged down Genesee,
dramatic head-turning cleave-less cleavage

resembling a blown-out tire along Highway 891,
though instead of miles of rabbit brush, broken glass,

Ron Paul stickers and bullet holes obscuring NO
LITTERING $750 FINE, memory fit padding out-blacking

the blackest roadside blackberries, the ones that show
their faces only as their leaves begin to yellow, curl.

Bra not showing its face, bra with a history like that 600-year-old
breast bag stuffed between floorboards in an Austrian castle,

raggedy sack of linen and lace that had lifted white-sand mountains,
milk chocolate double scoops. With sexy boost this land-less

landmass, this dollop-y desert dessert unloosed, shouting
she should never have got with that guy—never that bush,

those boys, that sequined sapphire dress, never this plunge-maker
plunging from a cherry red Camaro, bereft of what lifted its lace.

BREAST IMAGING'S

what they call it, but we all know
what they mean, that time of year

when our dangling darlings squished
till they resemble a sideways beanie a newborn

might sport on her journey home from the ICU.
Welcome to the room where radiance can cook you

to a cancerous cassoulet, and—voila!—lower the risk
of guzzling cyclophosphamide in hopes of squelching

mitosis. Hello, Selinia! You seem like a nice enough gal,
though I forgot, in the eight hundred days since I last held

you close, how much my breasticle resembles a pita sandwich
beneath this deli case where I consider each time I chose soppressata,

cappicola, not lentil croquettes, a cheery technician assuring me of ever-
improving treatments—every day in every way, and after, and after a long

beep I'm free to breathe, glance at the screen, at my pretty pair like two infant
galaxies, two baby solar systems with nary a hint of burgeoning planet, only

the swirling gas of weanlings, and yet, and yet, she is not saying, isn't
paid enough for tentative tumor news, lump lowdown, nor

does she have the degrees to suggest *further investigation*, to point
at a shadow, shadow as she pats my back, returns me

where my bra and sweater,
my kin and cosmos,
await.

SUMMONS AND PETITION FOR NAME CHANGE

Abelmosk. Abracadabra. Abruzzi. Absolute.
Bonzery. Bogan. Love's barometer. Bristly ballerina.
Choo-choo cherry sanctum. Cutie-cute caldera.
Dim sum-my dilberry. Down there Daiquiri.
Ear of Eden. Eminently Earthy. Empress Gensho.
Fandango-ing funnel. Fox foot. Flamingo.
Geranium in the Gate of the Gourd. Gentian's grin.
Hallelujah in the huckleberry. Ho-Ho-Kus.
Inner Inagaddadavida. Ink on the isthmus.
Jupiter's Big Red Spot. Un-January. Jambalaya.
Knit Kit. Kittewake. Kinnick-kinnick. Nether katzenjammer.
Laniferous lability. Hello Kitty lunch box. Lettuce cup asunder.
Mythic mouth. Mama's milk pan melts Emanuel. Maenadic moon.
Name It Not, Why Not? Nemorous nook. Nefertiti's niche.
O'Keefe. Unfrozen o-ring. Open the sunroom window.
Persimmon portal. Passworded pomegranate. Paisy-waisy.
Quaint Quiver. Quaking qat. Unquashable squab.
Rorschach-y rivulets. Ragmatical raven. Electric rabbit.
Susquehanna. Multi-syllabic sizzler. So strawberry.
Too much fun. Tell me another. Tisket. Tasket. Trisket.
Umbilical's prologue. My own undeniable. Under my undies.
Velvet-it's-not. Venus vector. Victory garden. Vroom-vroom.
Webbed Wednesday. Whipped up elixir. Wowie. Wha-wha.
Xizang. Xebec. Anti-xeric. Excitable raptor. Fringy xenon.
Yeti. Yangtze. Ygdrasil. *Yucca whipplei*. Yokozuma. Yapese dime.
Zounds-mound. Spangled zarf. Naughty zloty. Zerk gone berserk.

HOUSE OF MYSTERY

Here, where a girdle clothes-pinned to a clothesline
disappeared. Here, where a mother kept asking,

have you seen it? Have you seen my girdle? I hung it
on the line. Here, where a father decided every blessed

forsythia must be hacked to the nubbins. A cardboard box
teemed with laboratory frogs: when the first one died

the children were solemn; when the last one croaked
they took turns swinging its steel gray corpse at the pear tree

till one of its legs took hold to a sturdy branch. After
a downpour, mud-orange slugs worked their way

up the garage, beside *If you have an egg, get lost*
in pastel pink scrawl, There was burning meat,

an anti-Semitic who bought a house across the street
from a synagogue, and, by the way, did you know chrysalis

derives from the Hebrew *zahav*, meaning gold? Here,
where a father feared what would happen to his mind

if one of his children died. Here, where a girdle, without
fanfare or explanation, fluttered from a hapless sky.

WE FOUND MARTHA SILANO!

1.
Martha, as in Mary's sister. Old Testament Martha.
While Mary fawned over Jesus, Martha lugged a bucket,

took a seat at Jesus's feet. Obedient Martha, born
in the year of the ox. Martha, a scrub brush, bar

of Lava soap. Never loved Jesus because Jesus
hooked up with the Catholic Church, turned tail

on her parents for mingling too soon, but the diary's
locked, won't force open with a knife.

2.
The name *Silano*, her father used to say,
dates back eighteen generations, to Eppio

Silano, a Roman senator. *You're all descendants*
spreading pride like marinara on a hand-tossed pizza.

In a town where we were Guineas and Wops, he gave us
Josefina, Concetta, Madelina, Francesco, Antonio,

Vittorio, Anna Maria: *i radicci*. The mystery of the heavens
he could unravel, the untwisting/re-twisting dance

of DNA. The math behind orbits nuclear and celestial,
the why of a radio's static, but not the why

of a great-grandfather tending roses in a sanitarium.

3.

Sil, as in window, as in looking, wanting out. The sill
she tried to jump through. That sill, and seal, as in close.

La for lanthanum, from the Greek *to lie hidden*. A soft,
silvery metal easily tarnished. *La la la la*, it tunes

the orchestra. *La la la la* a mother's incessant cheery.
Ano, as in *anno*, sill of her years, all the rest of her years.

At the window she sang, sang *no*. Sealed in the no.
Sealed from knowing. Si and *no*. See La Know.

FLOWER GIRL

1.
She had wanted to be one
had always been one

girl with the yellow chin
girl who'd swooshed the buttercup

You must like butter you must
crocus tulip forsythia

on the teacher's desk inching out
googolplex   subset

lily of the valley fistful
for the hell of it for the smell of it

and dandelion's too their
monstrous taproots defying

the spade though mother insisted
she'd won that weedy war

2.
Regarded from a distance
with relative disinterest

then the special microscope
for carpels and locules

for epigenous versus hypogenous
She didn't think she would swim would

swim through the weekly quizzes
would she know for instance the tell-tale

signs of ranunculus   tricky as all
columbine and larkspur

He her professor told them tobacco
a pink trumpet   cashew related

to poison ivy it was all so new
it was all so not urban New Jersey

where she'd languished fifteen years
not knowing the phallic green finger

was a pulpit not seeing the spring
beauty though always loved the up

between patio cracks portulaca pink and yellow
like the Easter Bunny hid them the night before

3.
We'll be on the ground shortly but she didn't
want to   jettison us forward

past the mainland toward Hawaii
where monodelphous hibiscus

scarlet-ly rules the land   that one fused stamen
cheesy with pollen which in a musty Iowa lab

she stuck beneath a dissecting scope the better to
maybe I should drop like a drupe from a prickly stem

maybe she couldn't go this far past azalea
where a rose was not a rose but a tiny white bloom

lacking scent   climbed to the top
of Mount Kinabalu   scrambled up to see

the world's largest   *Rafflesia*   ruddy with donut disk
pronged like the suctioned feet of star fish

wholly parasitic   wholly making a living
off the vines of *Tetrastigma*

in the same way she had spread her haustorium
into mock orange honeysuckle lilac

ODE TO ARTICHOKES

O long and thick-stemmed chubby pinecones pyramid-stacked,
you're a posse of impossibly violet-tinged ghosts. Like instruments

of torture, some dark-aged throttling device—verdant, crustaceous—
you greet me like an off-track constellation of stalk-necked aliens.

I've heard you hail from the genus *Centaurea*, kin to all that stubborn
noxiousness—menacing, growth-stunting knapweed, horse-poisoning

star thistle, to the *God damn can't go barefoot in my own backyard.*
What we're eating when we eat you are the fleshy involucral bracts,

what our teeth glide against, resist, is the creamy-yellow
pulp of your innermost leaves, also known as the heart.

Born in Maghreb, you traveled to Egypt, graced the plates
of Romans and Greeks, then made your way down

to the southern Mediterranean where you met the Silanos of Napoli.
The French brought you west to America by way of the bayou,

while my tribe unleashed you on California, Castroville's
migrant workers now toting, in *canastas*, 70 million a year,

picking and tossing, picking and tossing, hustling down their rows
in The Artichoke Center of the World. O *Cynara cardunculus*,

peeling back your layers like returning to the Tuscan countryside
of my twenties, to an aging couple's stash of *Carciofi Sott'Olio*—

dipping crusty *pane* into choke-infused oil, savoring the succulent *couri*, that mauve-ish blush like a uterine shroud.

IF YOU COULD BE ANYBODY, WHO WOULD YOU BE?

And that's when she gave him her answer: Hapshepsut, the only female
pharaoh, who by the luck of her father's early death managed to rule

for twenty-two years. Or else, if not her, then the last person who died
with the secret recipe for embalming bodies, which wine, which incense,

when resin, when honey, when rubbing with grease, which thorny tree
of the Borage. That's when she gave him: or maybe Thomas Edison

on the day he invented the phonograph—telegraph tape, set at high speed,
emitting human speech. Paper speaking! Carbonate, bicarbonate, chloride,

sodium sulfite, who knows what else. Traveled to distant lands for their henna
and ochre. That's when she fessed up: Tanya Harding and Olga Korbut. Also,

Nadia Comeneci the day she received that perfect score. Also, she told him,
Botticelli's Venus. Does it have to be a person, she asked, or could she be

the pink shell? The creamy cockatiel, the yellow dewlap of the dewlapped lapwing?
The emu settling down in the dirt path for a late-morning nap? In that case, she said,

I'll be the light breeze, the glass of wine sweating in the late-June air; actually,
make that the 638 wineries of Washington State, every one of Klickitat County's

turbines slicing the wind through the cottony gospel of cottonwood fluff.
But she wasn't only Washington State; she was also a beaver's persistent teeth.

Gold, silver, bronze; floor, bars, or beam: who even remembers, and anyway
she'd rather be the chalk dust lifting after the champion raises her hand to signal

she's ready to vault. Or the moss between the patio bricks; a moose, an alpha wolf,
a stealth. Nothing camouflaged, nothing too outrageously flamboyant, nothing

requiring slaughter or stench. I've decided, she said, and that's when she gave him
that impossibly loose-lipped flower, white destined to dirty brown, to flop on the ground

for the girls to load their buckets for petal soup, cuz who'd give a camellia less
than a ten, who'd reject a blossom, though why hadn't she answered nobody

but nobody else, because really she loved her own aorta, her own prismatic ulnas,
was most content in her own cage, with the twenty-six bones of her foot. Not

platypoid, not tarantula-ized, just a smidgen spooked by King Tut's
bulbous belly, knocking knees, ghostly glowing teeth.

III.

WOLVES KEEP IN TOUCH BY HOWLING

and I keep in touch
with *you're pissing me off*

you're pushing my buttons
I'm not interested in rescheduling

Listen! Do you hear that?
That's my tongue licking

a laceration, a bloody metacarpal,
a fracture; that's my nasal baritone,

my *UUUUUU* unfurling your foothold.
Wolves keep in touch,

and I with my keen sense
sense extirpation (necrosis

suspected; necrosis likely). I scent;
I fang; I phalange; I from helicopters;

I for sport; I greedy chew my foot off;
I trickster; I snout. Wolves howl

in the smoothest of coats, guard hairs
shining, repelling the sopping.

Hackles raised, tail rigid, I'm fixing my stare
on the adamant, my ears to each leaf

as it falls.

TAUTAVEL MAN GLOSA

She's smart – for a woman.
I wonder how she got that way?
Just stay mum, pretend you're dumb.
That's how you come to be a lady.

This is what I learned today: the woman
was in her fifties. The man, twenty-five.
The rest—at least half—were children.
This is what the book said: *Tautavel Man*
is in fact the remains of twenty individuals.
The pelvis bone is rather feminine.
They found teeth, a fibula, a femur,
a humerus, a mandible. Cannibalism's
likely. Also, no fire (how gloomy).
She's smart – for a woman,

is how the song goes, the singer, burning
to be an engineer, keeps getting thwarted.
But she doesn't give up, full-well knowing
she's a bitch and a tart. Hired only
cuz the boss can pay her less. The lyrics
caustic, but Seeger croons like a sweet lady,
not a bitter femi-Nazi. Probably because
she's had to sing it so many times. The female
story of Tautavel: completely absent. Doesn't
appear on a single placard, poster, label.
I wonder how she got that way.

I wasn't going to write this poem. I said
to my sister, I want to write about Tautavel;
did you know he was actually a she?
But I don't want to pick that bone, the one
about language and gender, crimes of omission,
silences dictating culture. What man or woman's
pumped for that poem, or the one about scientists
convinced for eons humans evolved in Asia, not Africa?
Even Darwin took Seeger's advice, zipped up:
Just stay mum, pretend you're dumb.

I don't know: how hard would it have been
to call it Tautavel Village? Were they afraid
the truth would draw fewer crowds than a hairy
caveman wielding a spear? What up with positing
a feminine look to a bone? As it often does,
the things we say in silence astound me.
What should I tell my son and daughter,
when I bring them here? I'm sure we'll laugh
about the stuffed migratory hamster.
I almost didn't write this poem today.
That's how you come to be a lady.

APPROPRIATE INCONGRUITIES,

said the anthropologist; that's what distinguishes us
from Neanderthals—who would giggle when tickled,

who would smile when, say, a Levallois-pointed spear
sailed into the vat of rhinoceros stew, when Ogg tripped,

fell into the fire—but did not find delight in a kangaroo
disparaging the price of a Pabst, who would not have guffawed

at an elephant sitting on the marshmallow to keep from falling
into his cup of hot cocoa. Got their jollies instead

from Three Stooges antics—kicking, hair pulling, spear point
jabs, pants that split. *Repetitive expert tasks* rendered them adept

at knapping and hafting, worthless at asking *What do you call
a bee having a bad hair day? (A Frisbee!)* Theirs were stock,

as in *if it ain't broke*, their lexicon bereft of dumb blondes,
horses with long faces walking into bars, of riffing on *what*

stays in Vegas variants. Were there Neanderthal clowns?
Likely the need to diffuse tension existed, but a caveman

sporting plaid lapels, floppy hat, bulbous nose? Even if
there were no jesters, perhaps a tribal honker, a Groucho

galumphing around in mammoth-sized mammoth-skin galoshes?
Humor theorists conclude it takes an exceptional brain

to contrast instantaneously the disconnect between the kangaroo
and its unlikely yet plausible destination; its just-right incongruousness

like a Goldilocks cocktail of what's true, what's not: what we know
about *Macropus rufus* versus its ordering up a frosty cold one. Tip

the scales a tad too far—*Jupiter walks into a bar*, and pleasure
dissipates like a cumulonimbus into clear blue sky. Cognitively inflexible,

those not-quite-*sapiens* sapiens, their memory capacity substandard.
Unable to assimilate Sherlock Holmes and Dr. Watson on a camping trip,

pondering (astronomically, meteorologically, theologically, astrologically)
the stars, when what it all means (*You idiot!*) is that someone has stolen

their tent. No fossilized ukulele or banjo, no water-squirting bowtie
or *World's Best Jokes*, though who's to say a spear fashioned to look

like it's been lodged through the wearer's head might not one day be unearthed?

HOPE IS THE THING WITH

an important message, a pressing urgency
I reckon Hope's entitled to. Hope says *Hello,*

my dear, and it goes from there: *how are you,*
hope you're well, bit hot over here in Burkina

Faso, then Hope's done with asking after
my chargers, my panes, the windstorm nudging

my touch-and-go, has no time for me
or my closely-monitored percolations. Hope's

not perched; she's pouncing, marooned
to the tune of $4.5 million. But Hope's right:

her choosing me is a question she knows
she must answer. And big surprise: the Almighty

willed it, decided against her two sadistic aunts
because, Hope says, I'm different, won't sell

her dead mom's home to a Mr. Molson Steven
(though who can say for sure?). Hope's favorite

language? *Waiting to hear you soonest.* Hope's
solution: hide behind a bush so when I call

she can answer, or whatever (it's against the law).
Just like staying in the prison, says Hope before

signing off in the name of a nearby privilege,
in the name of *what I need from you is this.*

THE UN*TIED* STATES OF AMERICA

America, with your water-tower towns, your irrigation sprinklers,
your perpetual homage to Hopper. America, where if there's a river

there's a dam, and where there's a dam there's a peach grove, a flag
still there. America, where kids pry beer caps from the cooling asphalt.

America, a round of gunshots at three in the morning; the helicopters
circling, searching. America, falling asleep as the alarm starts beeping,

the wife having heard none of it, nothing since the chained dog finished
his aria at 2:37 am. America, a white tablet not exactly *tabula rasa*, on account

of the Lenapes and the Mohicans, on account of the Skagit and the wampum.
But America, the watercress in the oasis, the makeshift crosses. But America,

she outlived five husbands, though of course the questionable death
of the second, and the stolen cattle. America, a duel. America, a drowning.

America, an orchard. America, we are all going to college in diapers.
The prognosis is good, but first a year in Guatemala, a stint with the Nationals,

a frosty cold one. America, you're a Wells Fargo horse-drawn carriage.
America, a two-pack-a-day-Camel-unfiltered smoker. America,

the bees have taken over the foreclosures. America, where heroes sacrifice
flies. America, brave as a Cracker Jack. America, we will always pay more

for a view and take out. America, Lunestra-ed. Sonata-fied, all fired up
with popping The American Dream balloon. America, are you related

to anyone famous? America, more dessert than desert. America, *Tu casa es mi casa*. America, First Assembly of Quik-Mart, Un*tied* we Best Value.

America, you're an eagle of greed, an eagle of steel. America, Eat Now and Escape. America, you're a lake of illogic and thorns. O spacious skies,

Berkeley's a long ways from here. America, prepare to meet thy God of Lowe's. America, Assembly of Fitch. America, rest in peat and maggots

(the proof through the night). O outlet, o clearance, o slash, slash, slash. Bridges and brats, Dismal Nitch and pilings. America, too much faith

in plastic. America, you're a Sleep Country, a land of milk and money, $49.95 in a vein that will not vanish. America, in velvety red,

white, and blue, in solid-oak splendor, in Mahogany. America, you stupid, reckless lovely, rest in peace, thirty-four stems For a Limited Time Only.

EARLY SUNDAY MORNING GLOSA

Pity the planet, all joy gone
From this sweet volcanic cone;
peace to our children when they fall
in small war on the heels of small war.

Once home to 120,000 people, the Zone
of Alienation contains nearly 200 ghost towns.
On last count, 197 returnees were living
among barn swallows with eleven deformities—
swollen breasts, mottled plumage, mouths
that will not close—calling card of Strontium.
In the town of Pripyat, thirty high-rises
hold televisions and toilet seats too hot
to turn on, too hot to sit on;
pity the planet, all joy gone.

Be careful where you step, be wary
of the Safe Living Concept, selective
resettlements, revised delineations.
Reconsider that guided tour to sunny
Chernobyl; Plutonium's half-life's
24,400 years. Place a headstone
on eco-tourism, on Belarus's farmland,
wildflowers more toxic than you know.
The steam that wafted over
this sweet volcanic cone.

Some say it's our limbic system's
craving for hormones released
during brave and violent acts.
Some tell their people what's
making them sick is worry, stress.
But the birds with bent tails
don't know they're living
in a contaminated zone. Pity
the ones who suffer most: the small.
Peace to our children when they fall.

So many numbers, such dreary math—
easier to think of something else,
not the yearly thirty tons of spent
fuel rods with no safe place to go,
not the weasels with multiple heads.
Our grief stacks up like bricks, scores
of mold-ridden temples. Don't pray
to a saint, don't expect a burbling spring
to fix your damaged genes. No savior for
small wars on the heels of small wars.

LEONARDO DA VINCI'S GRAN CAVALLO

For seventeen years he sketched it,
made models from clay, built

a 20-meter deep casting pit, devised
a system of temporized furnaces.

His medium? 70 tons of molten bronze
to be poured, in less than three minutes,

into the mold of a 24-foot horse.
This he'd been commissioned to do

by the Duke of Milan, in honor
of the Duke's father, Francesco,

though Francesco disappeared
from the horse's back early on,

the artist so wrapped up in equine-
osity, in fortlocks and withers,

in coronets and hocks, in learning,
from bell makers, how best

to render a boisterous animal
rearing up unsaddled, unfettered,

unreined, though in the end the bronze
could not be melted into muzzle

or mane, though into the end,
in the Battle of Marignano,

the bronze he'd been promised
snatched away, hauled

through the Alps as seventy cannons.

EASTER DRAMA

Past Liquor World, past Pappy's BBQ, a red-tailed hawk
rapturously dive bombs a crow over 71B on the anniversary

of Christ's surprise visit to the tea-time gals to whom he proclaimed
in the fellowship of the kingdom there shall be neither man nor woman,

one of His many Ascension Day manifestations—puzzling, thespian-ly
pregnant. Twenty-one centuries later, plenty of post-Maundy Broadway,

bud-bursting serviceberry, potboiler Mayapple, bodice-busting lack
of poke. We're drowning in theatrics, raftless, the kids playing tag

in the grass while we search the banks for an unhistrionic patch of sand,
for an a-dramatic rock to throw. The girl with her shirt off.

The boy without his shoes. Maybe Jesus meant we're one and the same,
interchangeable, though of course not, so Barbie/Tonka, Dora/Diego.

My brother who swore off booze the same day his Savior rose from the dead
swears *tacos linguas* flex your lips, lucid your speech, make pronouncing

juego de dramatizacion a cinch, but I don't crave the stage or angst or tears,
anyone's piece of mind or tongue or lip. What I want is Vaudeville's

opposite, charge-neutral, as the coach coacher couched it, so take
your one-act, condense it down to ten minutes, then chuck it past

Don Tyson Boulevard, where they'll grind it down
to an unassuming meal for a small, defenseless pet.

SAINT CATHERINE OF SIENA

Short and frail. Sweet curmudgeon. Hairshirt clad. Bed of thorns.
When forced to eat, stuck a goose feather down her throat
till she puked. Willingly kept down only her daily communion wafer,

though for her friends she whomped up loaves of *foccacia, contucci,*
panforte, prayed for miraculous multiplicities—truffled *funghi*
pork loin *alla roman*a. Made an empty barrel gush Chianti, but her drink

of choice? Pus from the putrefactions, sores, and boils of the jailed
she freed with the gospel. From a great distance, sniffed out rancor:
three priests oversaw the confessions of her penitents.

I'm trying to make sense of her, her and her letters imploring her brother
to assume the armor of patience, referring often to afflictions, to the nectarous,
to the fruit of the soul, to great burdens lightening beneath *this most holy yoke.*

Attempting to imagine constantly courting pain, mutilated breasts and hips,
attempting to keep it in a 14th century context, not divorcing
the spiked whipping chains from the desire for immolation in the furnace

of salvation, that leap to faith akin to Adam's vault toward eternal
damnation, as all scab-munching saints bound toward the conundrum
cauldron (hating to love, following to lead, meeking it out to shine).

Snags in the fabric of accepting His mercy: (1) *great sins, great cathedrals*;
(2) why did it take Him eight billion years to arrive?; (3) respect for Buddhists,
Hindus, followers of the Koran; (4) opiate. And yet, and yet, who knows

the power of fighting one's fleshliness, one's appetite for, say, *porchetta,*
anatra all'arancia; who knows, maybe what oozes from pustules rivals
the custardy sweetness of *zuccotto.* Concetta Sabina Santaniello Tambini—

who at age 14 took the sacrament of confirmation at Our Lady of Sorrows Parish,
reminds me of the irrelevance of my pantyhose-with-a-run attempts at reasoning
out God—suggests Pascal's Gambit. But I'm already betting, I tell my friend,

though I'm not, keep dissing Him, about which dissing He shared with his
mystical, monastic wife: *this is that sin which is never forgiven, now or ever.* Infinite mercy
with a louse-sized caveat: surrender to be victorious; reject sin, befriend

the trespasser, be in the world but not of it, endless paradoxical paradise
like the colossal falling-leaves poncho my grandma Concetta would have knitted
if she knit, grabbing from a skein continuously transforming from yellow

to orange to red to brown, back to yellow again; slip 1 knit 1 *for you*
created my innermost being, knit me together in my mother's womb, row
upon row between the kindled and the damned, the now and the next.

THE ARCHITECT OF THE INEVITABLE

Assurance aborter

>Advocate of decay

Begotten breaker

>Boisterous blotter

Crusher of the coke-like rush

>Corrupter of the trance of can

Chaos concocter

>Dream dismantler

Discovery douser

>Sudden duster

Elegantly-erected eraser

>Excitement expunger

Effacer of the ferociously forged

>Giddily gotten gutter

Hacker of the handsomely honed

>Aha-moment hexer

Indeliblizer of the inky known

>Junker of gesso of gypsum

Kick-ass kenning killer

>Limberly-delivered leveler

Leisure liquidator

>Muffler of myriad maelstroms

Negater of the generate

>Obliterator of the opining pontificator

Concoction toppler

>Plunderer of the impulse to pulsate

Quasher of the waxing quail

>Ever-reveler of the unraveling

Spackling and speckles slayer

>Aspiration striker

Savorer of Destruction Soup
                    Tearer off-er of timpani at the dotted line
Undoer of the done
                    Devourer of chutzpah
Having Avenue Violator
                    Waker of the resolutely wow-drunken
Exhilarating sparkle x-er outer
                    Un-yesser of the fecund nod
Zany zing zapper

RIGHT ABOUT NOW

I'm ready to submerge myself inside
a Brugsmansia blossom, Solanaceae's

most pendulous, most Seussian bloom,
upside-down yellow deluge singing

like a fallen angel. Lemon-scented;
deadly. Peruvians feed them

to children to ward off unruliness,
their ancestors admonishing them

with hallucinations; shamans, ingesting
their pulverized seeds, diagnose disease,

prophesize, root out thieves. Slipping in
like slipping behind a pair of *Intimissimi,*

Victoria Secret's version of endowing
the unendowed. And endowed I'd be

with the mystery of medicine men, of medicinals
deemed, in today's world, toxic, of Machu Picchu.

If you can trademark a miracle, why not plunge
into fluted, into pendulousness

akin to what might be found in a great
grandmother's Sunday-best cupboard, shape

in which to serve an illustrious parfait; cascade
akin to a new-fangled phonograph—and I

the inquisitive dog, not merely pawing
at danger's door, but diving in.

THE POET IS THE PRIEST OF THE INVISIBLE

—Wallace Stevens

Dark-eyed, mysterious Meadowhawk,
the poet is the rabbi of the diaphanous,

scribe of the sheer, the barely-there
brief, pungi of the five o'clock shadow,

hint of rosewood and ghost. The poet
preaches a thin-barked willow sermon;

what she labors over is always prone
to sunscald, to scrutiny, its veins

visible through the skin. Gossamer
goddess, translucent muse, she lofts

a gauzy lug wrench toward the shadowy
freeway, where the alphabet—each of its

limpid clauses, each hyaline verb—
has once again broken down, needs a lift.

GOD IN UTAH

with apologies to Barbara Ras

As we gossiped at the hotel bar about ex-es and trances,
lechers and facelifts, God was in the oil, bathing

with the lightly-breaded scallops, resting on the bed
of squash risotto, making sure the mushrooms won't kill us.

As we debated coffee or no, God hovered between Hank
and his nametag as he tempted us with peanut brittle compote.

After we lay down our napkins, after we downed the last drops
of Pinot Noir, God followed us to the ladies, to a back room

where the good people of Salt Lake knocked back Manhattans,
obedient souls in crisp white collars, sensible oxfords. And God

was in the dark where the TV blared through the wall behind the bed,
where the moment the music crescendo-ed and the credits rolled,

a throbbing toe woke me; God in my left toe, God in the purple pillbox,
in the ibuprofen. I spied God the next morning in Nikki's nostrils,

in Keegan's fading acne; I tasted God in my breakfast burrito.
On the tour of Temple Square, God cracking up outside

the tabernacle, in stitches over the secret handshakes, especially
the Patriarchal Grip, God in his grandeur guffawing over barring

from worship the un-recommended. God defiantly breaking the rule
against unbridled laughter. God floating from garment to garment,

especially those escaping their clotheslines, drifting over rooftops,
finding safe harbor in a sweet gum or maple. God soaring over

the visitor center in the form of a falcon, but though a glossy pamphlet
suggested I reflect on the majesty of His creations as I stood beneath

the star-studded dome, the outstretched arms of an eleven-foot savior,
God could not be detected in the sound-muffling, dull-beige carpet.

God in the breezes from People's Freeway to Liberty Wells, God
in the stratification, all the way down to the very bottom, a couple

billion year's worth of sandstone, limestone, shale;
God in the volcanoes gracing that geologic layer cake

with ashy frosting; God in the 85% who live within fifteen miles
of the Wasatch Mountains; God in those who do not; God

in the scolecite, in the granite; God in the brachiopods
and the triops, in the millions of tons of monzonite quartz

hauled from a glacial trough in Little Cottonwood Canyon, where God
hangs out with the one-head sunflower, the everywhere aster.

WHAT FALLS FROM TRUCKS, FROM THE LIPS OF SAVIORS

South of Cincinnati two thousand cotechini slipped
from their crates onto a rush-hour roadway, rain

concocting a puke-red slush. When sweeping proved fruitless,
Jet Vacs rescued the route, funneling drivers toward the Ohio,

a drive now eerie with the ghosts of innards. Other drivers
have crashed into guardrails, drifted toward the center lane,

dumped delicatas and lava, brought to their doom dozens of goats,
passels of pullets, let loose a long, mucilaginous swath of glue,

dinged medians with thirty tons of Idaho spuds, unleashed
twelve million bees. Between the Jordan River and Damascus,

along the Visa Maris, in the early first century AD, along
with a quarter ton of Sunkist navels, Jesus pelted the populace

with *thou shalt have no other*, knocking out all communication
with Sabazius, the practice of flogging worshippers with vipers,

anointing them with bran and mud, which also put a swift halt
to the cult of Dionysus (tambourines clashing, goat guts bleating

for mercy, dripping blood bedabbled …), the cult of the dizzying
Pharaoh's Fury, Teacup Frenzy, cult of *he was not the God of libation –*

he was the libation. Sin washed up from the Sea of Galilee
like thousands of bags of Doritos, flummoxed beachcombers

gathering it up like netted tilapia, wolfing down each fluorescent
morsel like His sermons, each crunchy bite intoning *take up*

the whole armor of God. As if scrawled on the Tomahawk missile
sliding from its bed: *don't be afraid: believe.* Our Lamb of God

high-tailing it atop the rising waters at the Sheepshead Bay Yacht Club,
with alligators and Jello, with 600 piglets, 3,032 busted flour sacks.

Rome fully fallen, and like a La-Z-Boy uplifted in a flashflood torrent,
the apostles rising, Christianity catching on like PBR and beer nuts,

like Pop Rocks, Jesus juicing the citrus, and out gushes, with the pith
and the pulp, *Thou shalt not covet* and *Keep the Sabbath*, rendering

fatback into kielbasa, easing up on The Golden Rule long enough
to collect the miraculously-multiplying-from-a few-hundreds-

to-billions of fluttering-down dollars, looking the other way
because they're doomed, and besides, he's busy resurrecting

the glugging molasses, the tumbling hams, healing the wounds
of all who took a turn too fast, gashed their heads as a sugar beet load

overtook a swath of Dallas. Sweet Jesus! We're all going down
like a flotilla of entrails and skimmings. The bees cannot save us,

the bunnies cannot save us, the Savior cannot save us. We must make our way
in our own sticky, sanguineous stream, our own exploding sperm whale.

Decline and fall, decline and fall, toward the wrecking ball of eternal *who knows?*